A Gift for:

_____

From:

_____

HURRAHS AND HELPFUL HINTS

YOU GO, GRADUATE!

JOYCE VOLLMER BROWN

COUNTRYMAN

Copyright ©2001 by Joyce Vollmer Brown

Published by J. Countryman, a division of
Thomas Nelson, INC., Nashville, Tennessee 37214

Project Editor: Terri Gibbs

Unless otherwise indicated, all scripute quotations are from
the New King James Version of the Bible, © 1979, 1980, 1982, 1990
by Thomas Nelson, INC., publishers and are used by permission.

Scripture quotations noted NIV are from the
New International Version of the Bible, Copyright ©1983
by the International Bible Society and are used
by permission of Zondervan Publishers.

Designed by Left Coast Design, Inc., Portland Oregon

ISBN: 08499-9597-3

www.thomasnelson.com

Printed in the United States of America

To Ryan

Because I don't tell you enough how proud I am of the incredible young man you've become.

Contents

Accept Yourself

ever put yourself down. Doing so belittles your Creator. After all, He could have made you a billion different ways. He chose to make you just the way you are because He thought that was incredibly special. Remember, He never makes mistakes or does anything second best. You are a grade A, first class, top quality, deluxe model!

You formed my inward parts; You covered me in my mother's womb. I will praise You, for I am fearfully and wonderfully made.

PSALM 139:13-14

on't base your worth on how people value you. Base it on how much God loves you. There is no one in the world God loves more than you. He loves you as if you were the only person ever created. You are the apple of His eye (Zechariah 2:8).

Behold what manner of love the Father has bestowed on us, that we should be called children of God!

1 JOHN 3:1

Always be yourself
because the genuine article is better than an imitation.
Believe people will really like you once they get to know
the *real* you. Remember you are precious because you
are *unique*. You are the only person like you in
the whole world. No one else has your exact
thoughts, abilities, and experiences.

Just as each of us has one body with many members, and these members do
not all have the same function, so in Christ we who are many form one
body. . . . We have different gifts, according to the grace given us.

ROMANS 12:4–6 NIV

Your feelings about yourself largely determine your happiness and success. Focus on the positive in yourself as well as in others. Play positive movies in your mind of your performance in  future events. Rather than expecting to fail, picture yourself functioning successfully and happily.

Whatever things are true, whatever things are noble, whatever things are just, whatever things are pure, whatever things are lovely, whatever things are of good report . . .—meditate on these things.

PHILIPPIANS 4:8

Don't think less of yourself. Think of yourself less *often*. Recognize self-consciousness as pride and work to overcome it. Develop humility— the habit of thinking about others so much that you forget about yourself.

Remind yourself
that success isn't really about what you *accomplish*.
It's about who you *are*. True success isn't about *doing*;
it's about *being* who God wants you to be. He cares more
about your availability than your ability,
more about serving than striving, more
about attitude than achievement.

Whoever wants to become great
among you must be your servant.

MARK 10:43 NIV

15

G od has packed you full of potential miracles. The average person only achieves seven percent of his potential. Don't settle for average! Ask God to help you become all that He intended you to be.

[God] is able to do exceedingly abundantly above all that we ask or think, according to the power that works in us.

EPHESIANS 3:20

reat yourself as well as you would treat a friend. Like yourself in spite of your faults and enough to overcome them. Accept yourself (with your flaws) so you can accept others (with theirs).

Love your neighbor as yourself.

MARK 12:31

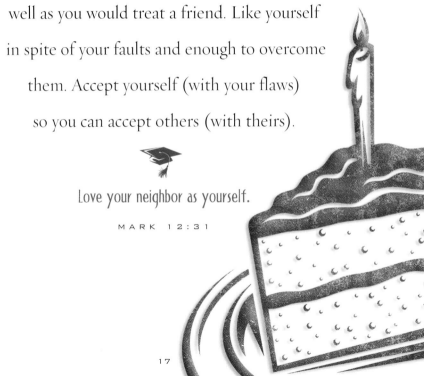

17

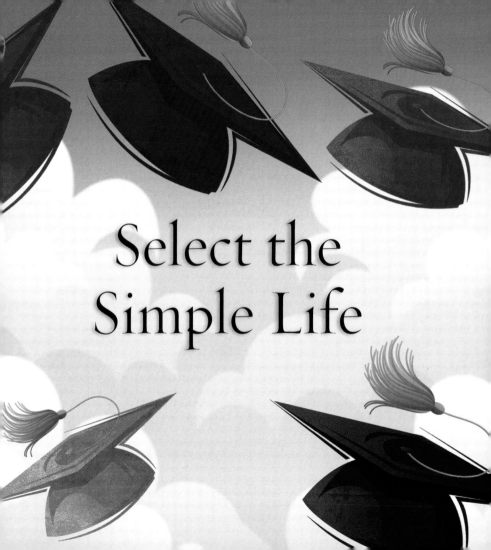

Select the Simple Life

Don't buy on the lay-awake plan. Spend less than you make. Distinguish between needs and wants. Ask God to keep your wants few. Remember lives based on *having* are less free than those based on *being*.

Better one handful with quietness than both hands full with toil and grasping.

ECCLESIASTES 4:6

20

Don't stuff so much stuff into your life that God gets lost in the shuffle. Own your belongings; don't let them own you. Hold possessions in your hand, not your heart. Enjoy your blessings, but love the Giver, not the gifts.

Do not lay up for yourselves treasures on earth . . .but lay up for yourselves treasures in heaven. . . . For where your treasure is, there your heart will be also.

MATTHEW 6:20–21

21

Don't sweat the small stuff. Learn to stop and recognize how small some of the things that upset you are. Develop the habit of asking, "Does this matter in the light of eternity?"

Set your mind on things above, not on things on the earth.

COLOSSIANS 3:2

Meditate on
the intricate details of God's creation:
the tiny food factories in tree leaves, the
engineering complexity of a bird's feather,
the unique design of each tiny
snowflake. NO detail in your
life is too small for God
to care about!

You know when I sit and when I rise;
you perceive my thoughts from afar.

PSALM 139:2 NIV

23

Worry is a

destructive habit. In effect, it is declaring

God is not worthy of our trust. We learn to be

anxious. We must teach ourselves not to be.

Peace I leave with you, My peace I give to you; not as the world gives do I give to you. Let not your heart be troubled, neither let it be afraid.

JOHN 14:27

24

Trust

that God *can* answer your

eeds and trust that He *will*.

Trust not only His power,

but also His love.

Believe God's

plans are good because His love,

His wisdom, and His power are

perfect. He wants the best for you.

He knows what's best for you. He has the

power to bring about the best for you.

As for God, His way is perfect.

PSALM 18:30

The secret to contentment is to believe that where you are, who you are, and what you have is right for you at this time. That it is all part of God's unique, individual, perfect plan for your life.

I know the thoughts that I think toward you, says the LORD, thoughts of peace and not of evil, to give you a future and a hope.

JEREMIAH 29:11

27

Help Yourself to
Good Health

Get enough sleep each day. Program your body clock by keeping a consistent sleep schedule, even on weekends. Getting outside during the day and following a relaxing, nesting ritual at night will help "set your clock." Avoid caffeine in the late afternoon or evening. Don't eat large or spicy meals late in the evening. Regular exercise (ideally five to six hours before going to bed) will also help you sleep better.

I will both lie down in peace and sleep; for You alone, O LORD, make me dwell in safety.

PSALM 4:8

Try to eat a rainbow of fruits and vegetables. The more variety, the better—different colors provide different nutrients. When making salads, use darker greens and reds. In general, choose fresh fruits and vegetables over frozen and frozen over canned.

Daniel then said to the guard . . . "Give us nothing but vegetables to eat and water to drink. Then compare our appearance with that of the young men who eat the royal food.". . . At the end of the ten days they looked healthier and better nourished than any of the young men who ate the royal food.

DANIEL 1:11–15 NIV

When possible, eat frequent small meals throughout the day rather than fewer large meals. This will make your metabolism more efficient and prevents blood sugar fluctuations—which are often accompanied by mood swings.

Everything that lives and moves will be food for you. Just as I gave you the green plants, I now give you everything.

G E N E S I S   9 : 3   N I V

Water is our most important nutrient. It makes up sixty percent of our bodies. Try to drink eight glasses a day. Water flushes out toxins, metabolizes stored fat, and maintains muscle tone. It makes you look and feel better!

He is like a tree planted by streams of water, which yields its fruit in season and whose leaf does not wither.

PSALM 1:3 NIV

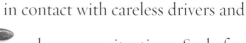

Driving is an enormous responsibility that can bring you in contact with careless drivers and dangerous situations. So, before you turn a car's ignition switch, buckle your seat belt and say a prayer. Ask God to guide you, protect you, and give you a calm, patient, and courteous attitude toward others.

Wisdom rests in the heart of him who has understanding.

PROVERBS 14:33

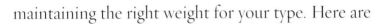

G od

created different body types. Work at

maintaining the right weight for your type. Here are

some tips: ◆ Eat on a regular schedule. ◆ Skipping meals

can actually cause weight gain. ◆ Few diets

work as well as long-term, healthy habits. ◆

Avoid sugar and you'll eventually lose your desire

for it. ◆ Eat slowly and savor your

meals. This will help you digest and

absorb food better and prevent overeating.

Sexual purity is a spiritual act of obedience. It deepens your self-respect, is crucial to your health, and increases the likelihood you will have a strong relationship when you marry. Because purity begins in the thoughts, guard your eyes and mind. Dress modestly so you don't cause others to have sinful thoughts.

Flee sexual immorality. Every sin that a man does is outside the body, but he who commits sexual immorality sins against his own body.

1 CORINTHIANS 6:18

Regular exercise
can make your heart healthier,
improve your cholesterol, prevent
bone loss, strengthen your
immune system, boost your
energy, elevate your mood,
enhance your self-confidence, increase
creativity, and control your weight.

Honor God with your body.

1 CORINTHIANS 6:20

Choose Joy

Don't absorb

the attitudes of those around you. Choose

your own. Happiness is a choice; it is also a habit.

Rejoice . . . in your youth, and let your
heart cheer you in the days of your youth.

ECCLESIASTES 11:9

Stop in the

middle of daily activities and remind yourself

that God is present right there beside you.

Savor the wonder of His nearness.

Seek the LORD while He may be found, call upon Him while He is near.

ISAIAH 55:6

 thankful heart is a happy heart. Never take blessings for granted because they've become commonplace. See how many things you can find to thank God for each day.

Sing and make music in your heart to the Lord, always giving thanks to God the Father for everything, in the name of our Lord Jesus Christ.

EPHESIANS 5:19–20 NIV

True

thanksgiving is not only expressing

thankfulness to God, but giving something back

of your time, energy, abilities, possessions, and love.

I will offer to You the sacrifice of
thanksgiving, and will call upon
the name of the LORD.

PSALM 116:17

Enjoy

the journey as much as the destination.

Hardly anything in the future will be as good or

as bad as we imagine it. So enjoy today for what

it offers without worrying about

or yearning for tomorrow.

This is the day the LORD has made,
we will rejoice and be glad in it.

PSALM 118:24

We usually find what we look for. Look for something good in people and situations around you. Expect the best—but remember that the best may not look exactly the way you pictured it.

To the pure, all things are pure.

You're the Best

No situation

is hopeless unless you are. Change is always

possible through you, around you, and

in you. A miracle could be on its way.

But remember: miracles don't always

happen instantly. Some come inch by

inch through years of prayer and obedience.

Be strong and take heart, all you who hope in the LORD.

PSALM 31:24

Live in the present. There is eternity in each moment if only we recognize it.

He has made everything beautiful in its time. Also He has put eternity in their hearts.

ECCLESIASTES 3:11

Be Real in Your Relationships

The essence of righteousness is having a right relationship with God and letting that relationship affect how you relate to other people. Make building and strengthening your relationships a top priority. Every day is a good day to love God and let Him love others through you.

If we love one another, God abides in us, and His love has been perfected in us.

1 JOHN 4:7

on't keep score in your relationships. Don't expect to be paid back for every kindness you do. Don't pay back for unkindness done to you. Remember, joy comes not so much from being loved as in loving.

Love suffers long and is kind; love does not envy,
love does not parade itself, is not puffed up.

1 CORINTHIANS 13:4

Don't expect perfection of yourself or anyone else but God. Remember Emerson's words: "There is a crack in everything God made." Encourage more and criticize less. Act more like a defense attorney than a prosecutor.

Don't hold onto anger. It will hurt you much more than whoever or whatever made you angry. You don't have to forget everything someone has done to forgive that person. All you have to do is give up your right to get even.

Be kind and compassionate to one another, forgiving each other, just as in Christ God forgave you.

EPHESIANS 4:32 NIV

Don't become tone deaf to your own voice. Be careful what you say and how you say it. Don't say it if you wouldn't write it and sign your name to it.

A man of knowledge uses words with restraint, and a man of understanding is even-tempered.

PROVERBS 17:27 NIV

When you must deal with a difficult person, mine for gold. Keep looking until you find some treasure—something you admire—then focus on that. And remember God may want to use that person to change *you*.

If it is possible, as much as depends on you, live peaceably with all men.

ROMANS 12:18

Loving unconditionally means loving regardless of others' faults and your circumstances. Put love in action even when it's not easy or convenient.

Greater love has no one than this, than to lay down one's life for his friends.

JOHN 15:13

Try to encourage and support others more than you try to impress them. Become a cheerleader. Give away compliments generously. Tell people you believe in them.

Pleasant words are a honeycomb,
sweet to the soul and healing to the bones.

PROVERBS 16:24 NIV

Manage Your
Money

Be the kind of employee you'd hire. Be punctual, honest, loyal, and ambitious. Don't gossip or spread discontentment. Get along with other employees.

Whatever you do, work at it with all your heart, as working for the Lord.

COLOSSIANS 3:23 NIV

60

D on't let

earning a living take the place of living.

Give your career your best efforts,

but don't let it consume you.

Do not wear yourself out to get rich; have the wisdom to show restraint. Cast but a glance at riches, and they are gone, for they will surely sprout wings and fly off to the sky like an eagle.

PROVERBS 23:4 NIV

Before you pay bills or pay yourself, pay the One you owe the greatest debt to and invest your wealth where you'll receive the greatest return—Eternity Unlimited.

Honor the LORD with your possessions, and with the first fruits of all your increase.

PROVERBS 3:9

Sacrifice short-term spending to accomplish long-term goals with a workable budget. Use these percentages of your take-home pay as guidelines:

10% God's work
17% transportation
11% personal insurance
6% health care
5% entertainment

24% housing
14% food
7% savings
6% clothing

Credit cards can spell financial disaster. Minimum payments are 90% interest; only 10% goes to the principle. Don't carry more than one card. Choose one with no annual fee and a low fixed rate. Never sign up for a card based on an introductory rate.

The rich rules over the poor, and the borrower is servant to the lender.

PROVERBS 22:7

Saving is the safest, surest way to financial security. Start saving now. If you invest $50 a month at 9 percent interest a year, in twenty years you'll have $33,394.

In forty years, you'll have $1,026,853.

The ants are a people not strong, yet they prepare their food in the summer.

P R O V E R B S   3 0 : 2 5

Purchasing a new car is rarely a good investment. As a general rule, new cars lose 25 percent of their value as soon as they're driven off the car lot. Add interest, if the car is financed, and it's not unusual to wind up owing more than the car is worth. Unless you can save enough to pay cash, it's usually wiser to buy a used car even if it ends up needing some repairs.

Better a handful with quietness than both hands full, together with toil and grasping for the wind.

ECCLESIASTES 4:6

Take good care of your car. ◆ Use fuel with proper octane requirements for the vehicle. ◆ Replace the oil and oil filter every 5,000 miles. ◆ Check the water levels, brake fluid, and power steering fluid every 5,000 miles. ◆ Check tire pressure once a month. ◆ Keep it clean—especially in winter climates where salt residues can corrode the body. ◆ Take it in for a checkup every 15,000 miles.

Learn the Secrets of Success

Time is one resource that can't be recycled. Use it wisely.

As John Wesley said, "Do all the good you can, by all the means you can, in all the ways you can, in all the places you can, at all the times you can, to all the people you can, as long as ever you can."

I must work the works of Him who sent Me while it is day; the night is coming when no one can work.

JOHN 9:4

Be less concerned about your *rights* and more concerned about your *responsibilities*. Ask yourself, "Do I see the needs I need met . . . but not the needs I need to meet?"

Let each of you look out not only for his own interests, but also for the interests of others.

PHILIPPIANS 2:4

As you rise each morning tell yourself, "I have great things to do today" There is a part in God's worldwide, eternal plan that won't be accomplished if you don't fulfill your assignment. You are indispensable to God's great plan!

We are His workmanship, created in Christ Jesus for good works, which God prepared beforehand that we should walk in them.

EPHESIANS 2:10

Remember the words of Edmund Burke: "All that is necessary for the triumph of evil is that good men do nothing."

◆ Make a difference.

◆ Take a stand.

◆ Fight in the Civil War of Moral Values.

Put on the full armor of God so that you can take your stand against the devil's schemes.

EPHESIANS 6:11 NIV

73

Much of the good done in this world is done by people who don't feel like doing it. Do more and you feel like doing more. Energy produces energy. Even when you don't feel like working, be grateful that you can.

He who gets wisdom loves his own soul;
he who keeps understanding will find good.

PROVERBS 19:8

pportunities

come dressed in overalls more often than tuxedoes.

Any work—no matter how menial— done

in love is divine work.

To do righteousness and justice
is more acceptable to the LORD
than sacrifice.

PROVERBS 21:3

The greatest things ever done on earth have been done little by little and little—little agents, little persons, little things, by everyone doing his own work, filling his own sphere, holding his own post, and saying, "Lord, what wilt thou have me to do?"

THOMAS GUTHRIE

Success is determined more often by concentration and perseverance than by talent or opportunity. Consider your work a self-portrait as well as a reflection on God. Mentally sign not only your name but Jesus' name to every piece of work you do.

By humility and the fear of the
LORD are riches and honor and life.

PROVERBS 22:4

Accept God's Grace

The measure you experience God's peace depends on the degree you understand and accept His grace.

You are deeply loved, totally forgiven, and completely accepted by God.

He loves you just as you are and all the time.

There is nothing you could ever do to make Him love you less.

He does not treat us as our sins deserve. . . . For as high as the heavens are above the earth, so great is his love for those who fear him.

PSALM 103:10-11 NIV

A ccept God's

unconditional love and forgiveness unconditionally.

Don't attach your own restrictions. Grace

is absolutely free (or it's not grace).

I do not set aside the grace of God, for if righteousness could
be gained through the law, Christ died for nothing!

GALATIANS 2:21 NIV

Even when you fail, you are still precious because of the ultimate price Christ paid for you. Refuse to fight the never-ending battle to prove your worth to God, others, or yourself. Remember Christ's final words on the cross: "It is finished."

In all these things we are more than conquerors through Him who loved us.

ROMANS 8:37

D on't use past failure as an excuse to fail again. The Holy Spirit convicts you of sin and helps you turn from it. When Satan tries to condemn you and convince you that you're a hopeless case, ignore him. Listen to the Holy Spirit.

Remember,
you haven't lost until you quit. The God who made

you is willing and able to make you more like Him. Even

if you fail over and over, you can gain victory with His help.

He won't give up on you if you don't give up on Him.

If anyone is in Christ, he is a new creation;
the old has gone, the new has come!

2 CORINTHIANS 5:17 NIV

As a wise person once said, "When you sin, practice the 3 R's: repent and resolve not to repeat." Don't dwell on your mistakes. Rather than staring backward saying, "If only . . . ," look forward and say "Next time . . ." Remember, this world is merely a training camp for the next.

Serve God not because of what He will do to you if you don't, but because of what He has already done for you. What you have freely received—grace and forgiveness—freely give to others.

Be kind to one another, tenderhearted, forgiving one another, even as God in Christ forgave you.

EPHESIANS 4:32

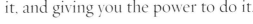 emember,

grace is more than forgiveness. It not only frees

you from what you were; it also frees you

to be all you were meant to be.

Grace is God asking you to do

something, helping you want to do

it, and giving you the power to do it.

Stretch Your Faith

Don't let

things that seem to demand *immediate* attention sap all

your time and energy so that you neglect things that

are truly *important*. Take time to feed your soul.

In quietness and confidence
shall be your strength.

ISAIAH 30:15

on't be a
religious Lone Ranger. Allow other Christians
to pray for you and encourage, inspire, and help you.

Let us not give up meeting
together, as some are in the
habit of doing, but let us
encourage one another.

HEBREWS 10:25 NIV

◆ Slow down.

◆ Rather than trying to go faster and farther, focus on going deeper.

◆ Downscale material goals and upgrade spiritual ones.

◆ Be content with what you have, not with what you are.

Turn my eyes away from looking at worthless things, and revive me in Your way.

PSALM 119:37

ake a
spiritual inventory every now and then:

Are you struggling with the same
hang-ups you were a year ago?

Has your heart become softer?

Your discipline firmer?

Your devotion deeper?

This is what the LORD Almighty says:
"Give careful thought to your ways."

HAGGAI 1:7 NIV

Who you were yesterday does not have to determine who you become today. Christ has the power to make all things new. With His help you can break sinful habits and be healed of crippling thoughts and attitudes.

Thanks be to God, who gives us the victory through our Lord Jesus Christ.

1 CORINTHIANS 15:57

Faith won't grow unless it is used. Live your life on the growing edge—take godly risks. Do some things you're afraid to do. Don't make the mistake of never making any mistakes.

The righteous are as bold as a lion.

PROVERBS 28:1

95

The decisions you make today will take you a few steps closer to or farther away from God; toward godly or ungodly character. Every day you move in one direction or the other by your thoughts, words, actions, and deeds.

Present yourselves to God as being alive from the dead, and your members as instruments of righteousness to God.

ROMANS 6:13

Set

your will over your emotions:

- Live as if you have courage until you do.
- Praise God when you don't feel like it.
- Love your neighbor when he is unlovable.
- Forgive the unforgivable.
- Hope when the days are dark.
- Trust when answers seem impossible.

Practice Prayer

emember God is never too busy to listen, help, and guide. He speaks to His children all the time—through people, circumstances, music, His Word, and that quiet voice inside. Learn to listen.

Let the hearts of those rejoice who seek the LORD!
Seek the LORD and His strength.

PSALM 105:3-4

here is a time

and place for prayer—anytime, anywhere.

Make the most of spare moments: talk to God when

you're standing in line, riding in a car,

doing chores, taking

a shower, or

exercising.

Pray continually.

1 THESSALONIANS 5:17 NIV

ive time

every day to the One who has given you eternity!

Make an appointment to meet with Him. If you don't

set a time for prayer, you probably won't get to it. Follow

Corrie ten Boom's advice to make prayer your steering

wheel—not your spare tire.

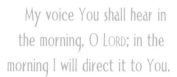

My voice You shall hear in
the morning, O LORD; in the
morning I will direct it to You.

PSALM 5:3

T

hank God before He answers because you know He will. He answers every prayer. Of course, the answer isn't always, "Yes." Sometimes it's "No," and sometimes it's "Not yet." Don't argue. Don't try to convince Him to answer your way. Trust Him to do what's best.

He will be very gracious to you at the sound of your cry; when He hears it, He will answer you.

ISAIAH 30:19

Pray and wait, but work while you wait. Jesus told us we could move mountains if we had faith. But He never said we wouldn't need a shovel, too. As the German proverb says, "Pray as though no work would help and work as though no prayer would help."

But if we hope for what we do not yet have, we wait for it patiently.

ROMANS 8:25 NIV

Explain your problems to God until you understand them better. Pour out your feelings. You can't shock God. Don't worry about including too many details or repeating yourself. He's never too busy to listen, and He never gets bored.

Trust in Him at all times, . . . pour out your heart before Him; God is a refuge for us.

PSALM 62:8

Pray honestly

You can't fool God. If you're not sorry for

sinning, ask Him to help you see sin the way

He does. If you're not ready to accept

His will, ask Him to make you

willing to be willing.

When you pray for change, be willing to be changed. The ultimate goal of prayer is not getting more of what you want, but rather becoming more of who God wants you to be.

Search me, O God, and know my heart;
. . . and lead me in the way everlasting.

PSALM 139:23-24 NIV

Live God's Truth

Don't be content to know the truth — be the truth. Live what you know. Behave what you believe. At the end of each day ask yourself, "What have I done today that glorified God? What have I done that didn't?"

Teach me to do your will, for You are my God;
Your Spirit is good. Lead me in the land of uprightness.

PSALM 143:10

The only way to know God is to spend time with Him. As you get to know Him better, it will become easier to trust Him. Once you learn to trust Him, it will be easier to obey Him. Obeying Him will draw you closer to Him.

If anyone loves me, he will obey my teaching.

JOHN 14:23 NIV

God never changes.

Neither do His standards. What is considered proper

according to society may change with each passing

trend, but God's law remains exactly the same.

Your word is a lamp to my feet
and a light to my path.

PSALM 119:105

God forgives sin; He does not undo it or prevent the consequences. Sin always costs something. The next time you're tempted, remind yourself that giving in to sin is like buying something on credit—you always pay for it later, with interest.

My hope is in you. Deliver me from all my transgressions.

PSALM 39:7-8

113

Decide to be strong. Discipline yourself. The happiest people in this world are often the best disciplined. But don't try to handle spiritual battles alone. Depend on the Holy Spirit's power whenever you face temptations.

For the LORD will be your confidence and will keep your foot from being snared.

PROVERBS 3:26 NIV

Play your life for the praise of the Coach—not the cheers of the crowd. Don't worry about what others think of you. Worry about what others think of Jesus because of you.

Am I now trying to win the approval of men, or of God? . . .
If I were still trying to please men, I would not be a servant of Christ.

GALATIANS 1:10 NIV

Y ou can't put your hand in God's hand until you let go of everything else. Surrender all to gain more. Don't settle for your own sprinkle of blessings when God wants to shower you. Remember those who leave the choices to God wind up with God's choicest gifts.

Because Your lovingkindness is better than life, my lips shall praise You.

PSALM 63:3

Discover God's will in the Bible, through prayer, and from wise advisors. Turn your will toward His. Your willpower and His supernatural power will make a winning combination!

I will instruct you and teach you in the way you should go; I will guide you with My eye.

PSALM 32:8

Notes of congratulations fror

mily and friends: ⎯⎯⎯⎯⎯⎯